A SHORT BIBLE STUDY

I0554891

The
NAME
OF GOD

LEARNING THE
Personal Name
BEHIND THE TRANSLATION
"THE LORD" IN
Scripture

DEANNA MUNGER

Scripture quotations taken from the (NASB®) New American Standard Bible®, Copyright © 1960, 1971, 1977, 1995, 2020 by The Lockman Foundation. Used by permission. All rights reserved. www.lockman.org.

This book was edited by Pamela Emerson, Daniel Munger, and Linda Munger. It was formatted by Julie B. Abels. Cover design by Deanna R. Munger.

Reading Chair Press: Austin, TX

BISAC Codes: REL006000, REL006700
ISBN 978-1-962428-00-2 (paperback)
ISBN 978-1-962428-01-9 (e-book)

Contents

Chapter One

God Reveals God's Name

¹⁴ *God said to Moses, "I AM WHO I AM"; and He said, "Thus you shall say to the sons of Israel, 'I AM has sent me to you.'"* ¹⁵ *God, furthermore, said to Moses, "Thus you shall say to the sons of Israel, 'The LORD, the God of your fathers, the God of Abraham, the God of Isaac, and the God of Jacob, has sent me to you.' This is My name forever, and this is My memorial-name to all*

generations...."

Exodus 3:14-15, NASB

Have you ever wondered why the Bible sometimes puts the word "LORD" in small caps, and whether it means anything? It definitely does mean something! It represents the personal name of God. "God" is a title rather than a name, but God has a proper name. Look at verse 15 above. God says to tell Israel that God is "the LORD, the God of your fathers..." with "the LORD" in the small capitals format, which represents God's personal name.

The personal name of God appears from the very beginning of the Bible narrative (Gen. 2:4 is the first instance). This name appears throughout the text of Genesis, but in the story of Scripture God doesn't actually reveal the name until the second book of the Bible, Exodus. In Exodus 3, we read the story of

God revealing God's name, so that's where we'll begin.

In Chapter 1 of this book, we'll first study the story of God's revelation of God's divine name in Exodus 3. Then in Chapter 2, we'll look at the history of how the name of God came to be written as "the LORD" in our English Bibles. Finally, in Chapter 3 we'll consider what it means to us and in what way we should use the name of God.

God Calls Moses

At the beginning of the book of Exodus, the people of Israel are enslaved and oppressed (Ex. 1). God sees their suffering and determines to rescue the people. God's first action is to commission a representative, Moses.

Moses is a Hebrew, a member of the people of Israel, but a Hebrew who has been raised as an Egyptian—in the house of Pharaoh, no less!

Moses was supposed to be killed at birth, but through a fascinating series of events he is saved and adopted into the Egyptian royal household. Then as an adult, Moses suddenly switches sides, killing an Egyptian who was abusing an Israelite. Once people start discovering what he has done, Moses goes on the run to avoid a death sentence, fleeing into the desert. There he marries and makes a simple life as a shepherd, away from the Egyptians and the Israelites. Moses spends years in the desert until he has a crucial encounter with God.

The Burning Bush That Isn't Burning Up

¹ Now Moses was pasturing the flock of Jethro his father-in-law, the priest of Midian; and he led the flock to the west side of the wilderness and came to Horeb, the

mountain of God. ² The angel of the LORD appeared to him in a blazing fire from the midst of a bush; and he looked, and behold, the bush was burning with fire, yet the bush was not consumed. ³ So Moses said, "I must turn aside now and see this marvelous sight, why the bush is not burned up."

⁴ When the LORD saw that he turned aside to look, God called to him from the midst of the bush and said, "Moses, Moses!" And he said, "Here I am." ⁵ Then He said, "Do not come near here; remove your sandals from your feet, for the place on which you are standing is holy ground." ⁶ He said also, "I am the God of your father, the God of Abraham, the God of Isaac, and the God of Jacob." Then Moses hid

his face, for he was afraid to look at
God. (Exodus 3:1-6, NASB)

As Moses is living his shepherd life, he sees a
strange sight: there is a blazing fire, but it is
a fire that does not consume any fuel. Moses
decides to stop his work to investigate, to see
this "marvelous sight." Moses turns aside and,
perhaps because he was willing to turn aside and
look, God speaks to him.

God is speaking "from the midst of the bush"
(verse 4) so we understand that God is manifest
in this blazing fire that does not consume the
bush. This fire is the holy presence of God.
How does God introduce who God is? God's
first introduction here is as the God of Moses'
ancestors, Abraham, Isaac, and Jacob. This is not
one of the gods of Egypt—this is the God Moses
knows from his Israelite heritage.

In the next verses, we learn that God has heard
the people crying out from their suffering and

enslavement in Egypt. God's plan is to rescue the Israelite people by sending Moses to Pharaoh to collect the Israelites and lead them out of slavery. What a great plan, right?

Well, Moses has some concerns! Pharaoh is a very powerful king, whereas Moses is a disgraced fugitive. Moses had fled the country after murdering an Egyptian, so he is not going to be well-regarded by Pharaoh. And Pharaoh likes having the Israelites for slave labor. Pharaoh is frightened because the Israelites have become so numerous and strong (Ex. 1:8-10), but having them as slaves is very useful to him. Entering Egypt and telling Pharaoh to let the people go is not going to be an easy job. Not only is it going to be difficult, it's also going to be dangerous! So Moses starts objecting.

What Name Shall I Tell Them?

Moses' first question is, "Who am I, that I should go to Pharaoh, and that I should bring the sons of Israel out of Egypt?" (Ex. 3:11). God's answer is unexpected. When Moses says, "Who am I?" the response from God is, "I'll be with you." Apparently Moses doesn't need to worry about his own qualifications—he just needs to know God is with him. Since God's presence is the key, then the point is really who *God* is, not who Moses is. Moses' next question, therefore, is logical: it's something like, "Well then, who are YOU?"

> "...[10] Therefore, come now, and I will send you to Pharaoh, so that you may bring My people, the sons of Israel, out of Egypt." [11] But Moses said to God, "Who am I, that I should go to Pharaoh, and that I should bring the sons of Israel out of Egypt?" [12] And He said, "Certainly I will be with you, and this shall be the sign to you that it is I who have sent you: when

you have brought the people out of Egypt, you shall worship God at this mountain."

[13] Then Moses said to God, "Behold, I am going to the sons of Israel, and I will say to them, 'The God of your fathers has sent me to you.' Now they may say to me, 'What is His name?' What shall I say to them?" (Exodus 3:10-13, NASB)

Moses argues that he'll have to tell the Israelites a real name for God. Here we might ask, "Isn't God's name… '*God*?'" But God is not a name—instead it is a title. "God" is the English word for a divine being. We use it to describe gods such as Zeus, the Greek god of thunder, and Ra, the Egyptian sun god. We capitalize "God" when we are referring to the God of Abraham, Isaac, and Jacob, but it is still a title.

In Hebrew, the equivalent word for God is El or Elohim (Elohim is the plural of El, but it is used as a singular due to a grammatical quirk of Hebrew). It is a title that is used to refer to any god—to the Israelite God or to the gods of the nations.

So Moses wants a proper name—a personal name, not just the word for a god. Moses says the Israelites will demand a name. Maybe he thinks his Egyptian upbringing will bias the Israelites against him and just saying he is from "the God of Abraham, Isaac, and Jacob" won't be enough. But there may be another reason Moses wants to know God's name.

The other nations surrounding the Israelites during this time would use names as a means of exercising power over their gods. They believed knowing a god's name would allow them to use an incantation that included the god's name to *make* the god respond. Knowing a god's name was a key to gaining power over that god. This makes us wonder: did Moses think he could gain some power over the Israelite God by knowing God's name?

I AM WHO I AM

Either way, Moses says, if you're going to send me, I'm going to need your real name. God answers Moses and provides a name, though it's a rather odd one:

> ¹⁴ God said to Moses, "I AM WHO I AM"; and He said, "Thus you shall say to the sons of Israel, 'I AM has sent me to you.'" ¹⁵ God, furthermore, said to Moses, "Thus you shall say to the sons of Israel, 'The LORD, the God of your fathers, the God of Abraham, the God of Isaac, and the God of Jacob, has sent me to you.' This is My name forever, and

this is My memorial-name to all generations...." (Exodus 3:14-15, NASB)

God says something cryptic, and a little hard to translate. It could be rendered "I am who I am," as we see above, or "I am what I am," or "I will be what I will be." God's statement contains the idea of "I'm beyond your comprehension." It also has a strong sense of God existing without dependence on anything. God isn't contingent on anyone or anything—God just *is*. God always *has been*, and God always *will be*.

Notice that God is not worried about giving out a name. God isn't giving away power, and God certainly won't be controlled by an incantation invoking God's name! But God *is* generous, giving Moses the divine name with instructions to share it. God shows something true about God's nature in this revelation.

We remember that God appears here as a fire. But it is not a normal fire, it's a fire that doesn't consume anything. God's fire doesn't require fuel or any source. What might that mean? My friend Dr. Daniel Napier, a brilliant teacher, calls the "unfed fire" here a "conceptual image." A conceptual image is a picture or scene that communicates a concept. When we think about what ideas are implicit within the image, we learn more about what is being taught (please see "Sources" at the back of this book for source information on this quote and idea from Napier's forthcoming publication).

Here, God is communicating not only through words, but also through the conceptual image of the fire. God appears as a fire that is not contingent on anything, a fire that doesn't depend on anything outside itself to exist. Fire usually *is* contingent on fuel and oxygen. The energy of the fuel supplies the energy of the fire. But this fire in the burning bush isn't burning any fuel. It exists without needing to come from anywhere but itself. The image of the burning bush reveals something about God that aligns in meaning with God's name. The fire is non-contingent, depending on nothing else for existence, just as God is non-contingent. God's being comes only from God, which is why God says, "I AM WHO I AM."

Name? What Name?

But wait, we might ask, where is the name here? God says, "this is my name" (verse 15), but do you see a proper name in that paragraph? It is there, but it's hidden. God's name is the word in Hebrew that is rendered as "the LORD" in English in verse 15:

> "Thus you shall say to the sons of Israel, '**The LORD**, the God of your fathers, the God of Abraham, the God of Isaac, and the God of Jacob, has sent me to you.'

This is My name forever, and
this is My memorial-name to
all generations...." (Exodus 3:15,
NASB, emphasis added)

The name itself, written as "the LORD" in small
caps formatting in English, is four letters in
Hebrew that form a proper name. These letters
are transliterated (written in our alphabet rather
than the Hebrew alphabet) as *YHWH*:

"Thus you shall say to the sons
of Israel, '[*YHWH*], the God of
your fathers, the God of Abraham,
the God of Isaac, and the God
of Jacob, has sent me to you.'
This is My name forever, and
this is My memorial-name to
all generations...." (Exodus 3:15,
NASB, emphasis added)

This four-letter name is sometimes called the Tetragrammaton, which comes from the Greek words for "four letters." It is literally translated as "He is" or "He will be." Because of God's statements in verse 14, "I AM WHO I AM" and "Thus you shall say to the sons of Israel, 'I AM has sent me to you,'" we think of the meaning of God's name as "I AM."

I am the LORD

What is the significance of God revealing God's name at this time in Israel's history? To consider this question, let's look at another scene, when Moses is deeply discouraged and convinced that the rescue of the people is never going to happen. Moses comes to God to complain. Moses says, "This plan isn't working! It's only making everything worse!" We can relate to that, can't we? Problems arise all the time and solutions come so slowly. It's hard to navigate the difficulties and setbacks of life, even when God is calling you to do something.

God's answer to Moses' complaint is illuminating.

> 22 Then Moses returned to the LORD and said, "O LORD, why have You brought harm to this people? Why did You ever send me? 23 Ever since I came to Pharaoh to speak in Your name, he has done harm to this people, and You have not delivered Your people at all."

> 6 1 Then the LORD said to Moses, "Now you shall see what I will do to Pharaoh; for under compulsion he will let them go, and under compulsion he will drive them out of his land."

2 God spoke further to Moses and said to him, "**I am the LORD;** 3 and I appeared to Abraham, Isaac, and Jacob, as God Almighty, **but by My name, LORD, I did not make Myself known to them.** 4 I also established My covenant with them, to give them the land of Canaan, the land in which they sojourned. 5 Furthermore I have heard the groaning of the sons of Israel, because the Egyptians are holding them in bondage, and I have remembered My covenant. 6 Say, therefore, to the sons of Israel, 'I am the LORD, and I will bring you out from under the burdens of the Egyptians, and I will deliver you from their bondage. I will also redeem you with an outstretched arm and with

great judgments. [7] Then I will take you for My people, and I will be your God; and you shall know that **I am the LORD** your God, who brought you out from under the burdens of the Egyptians. [8] I will bring you to the land which I swore to give to Abraham, Isaac, and Jacob, and I will give it to you for a possession; **I am the LORD.**'" (Exodus 5:22–6:8, NASB, emphasis added)

The first thing we notice is that God is not at all exasperated at Moses and his complaining! God is compassionate to Moses and answers his complaint. God is saying, "I will rescue my people. It will happen." Why? Because "I am the LORD." But... why is that a reason? God's *action* to rescue the people is based on God's *character*. And God's name represents God's character.

Here, God uses it to explain that God will rescue because that's who God is.

God has now made God's nature known to them in a new way, a way God has never done before. God says, "by My name, LORD [*YHWH*], I did not make Myself known to them" (verse 3). And look at how God emphasizes God's name. Read back through the passage—how many times does God say, "I am the LORD?" Whenever we notice repetition in Scripture, we look for what is being emphasized. God is emphasizing God's identity as *YHWH*, the Lord, the great I AM.

Let's return to the question: What does it mean that God reveals God's name at this particular time? The scene at the burning bush is the beginning of God's rescue of Israel. God uses the unfueled fire and God's revelation of the name *YHWH* to tell Moses, and us, something important about God: that God is not contingent. God has no dependence on anything but God's own self—not Pharaoh, not the armies of Egypt, not even Moses. God will rescue the descendants of Abraham, Isaac, and Jacob as God promised. This revelation begins the story of the Exodus, a story that will continue to reveal God's nature and character.

God reveals the name *YHWH* at the beginning of God's rescue project. God's claim about the rescue is that being the LORD means God will hear the people and deliver them. God will act in love and power. God will take them as the people of the LORD and bless them. This is the character of *YHWH*, the LORD.

Moses doesn't need to learn God's name so that Moses can use it in an incantation to compel God to act. This isn't a story of Moses tricking God so that Moses can get his wishes granted, is it? God will reveal God's name to Moses out of love, and rescue the people out of love. The revelation of God's name and the rescue of

God's people both flow from the love of God. That is the nature of *YHWH*.

What does it mean to us that God reveals God's proper name in Scripture? What does it mean to us that God is a non-contingent being? Before we discuss these questions, let's pause and discuss how God's name is written in our English translations of Scripture.

Key Scriptures for Chapter 1: "God Reveals God's Name"

Exodus 3:1-15
Exodus 5:22-6:8

Questions for Thought or Discussion:

1. Why do you think Moses asked to know God's name? What would he gain by knowing it?

2. When have you felt unqualified for something you needed to do? When have you asked, "Who am I to do this?"

How would it change your feelings to consider God's presence with you as more important than your feelings of being unqualified?

3. How would you explain the meaning of the fire that does not consume fuel? How does it illustrate God's nature?

4. What does the name of God, YHWH, or "I AM," mean to you?

Chapter Two

The Tetragrammaton and "the LORD"

¹⁹ *And He said, "I Myself will make all My goodness pass before you, and **will proclaim the name of the LORD before you**; and I will be gracious to whom I will be gracious, and will show compassion on whom I will show compassion."*

⁶ *Then the LORD passed by in front of him and proclaimed, "**The LORD,***

the LORD **God***, compassionate
and gracious, slow to anger, and
abounding in lovingkindness and
truth;* [7] *who keeps lovingkindness
for thousands, who forgives iniquity,
transgression and sin; yet He will
by no means leave the guilty
unpunished, visiting the iniquity of
fathers on the children and on the
grandchildren to the third and fourth
generations."*

*Exodus 33:19; 34:6-7, NASB,
emphasis added*

G od revealed the name *YHWH*, the
Tetragrammaton as it is sometimes
called, to Moses at the burning bush (Ex.
3). God was making an important revelation
in the divine name of *YHWH*. When God
showed God's glory to Moses in Exodus 34:6-7

(above), God did so by proclaiming the name and the character of God. The name of God represents God's compassion and grace, God's lovingkindness and forgiveness, and God's justice. That's how important the divine name is—it represents the nature and character of God!

Why Don't We See *YHWH* in the Bible?

God's name is used throughout the Hebrew Scriptures, what we call the Old Testament. They were originally written in Hebrew and were the Scriptures of the Hebrew people, the Israelites. But you'll notice that when we read these Old Testament passages in our English translations, we don't see anything that looks like *YHWH*.

Look at verse 19, above. God says "I… will proclaim the name of the LORD before you." In the Hebrew text that phrase reads "I will proclaim the name of *YHWH* before you." So why is it written as "the LORD" in English? Why doesn't the English translation have anything that looks like a proper name?

The answer is a fascinating bit of translation history (at least I think it's fascinating!). As we follow the translation story, we'll learn a little about how Hebrew text works, where the name "Jehovah" came from, and why "LORD" is used to represent the Hebrew *YHWH*.

The Hebrew Text

At the time the text of the Hebrew Bible was finalized, Hebrew was written in all consonants—the vowels were just implied. Scholars also debate whether there were spaces between the words, but apparently by the period of the Exile when the text was finalized, there were some spaces between words, so spaces are included here. To give an example in English, it would be like reading this:

MRY HD LTTL LMB

You could figure it out, right? But, not as easily as with vowels! (Hebrew doesn't have the word "a" either—I didn't leave it out only because it was a vowel.)

Later, a group of Jewish scholars, the Masoretes (sixth to tenth century AD), added vowels to the text to increase clarity. But they didn't want to *change* the sacred text. In fact, they wanted to be totally clear about what was original and what they were adding, so they added the vowels as symbols above and below the consonants. The vowels are called "pointing," because they are mostly made up of dots (you'll see these dots when I show some Hebrew text below). It would be almost like this:

M^{a}RY H^{a}D L^{i}TTL^e L^{a}MB

However, when they came to the name of God, they did something special because of the holiness of the divine name. Over the generations, Hebrew readers stopped pronouncing the name of God, considering it too sacred to risk profaning it by speaking it aloud. Instead, when they came to the letters *YHWH*, readers would substitute *Adonai*, the Hebrew word for "lord," saying it aloud instead of God's name. *Adonai*, like our English word "lord," is a word that can be used as a synonym for God or as a title for a human lord or master.

When the Masoretes were adding vowels to the name of God, they didn't add vowels that might connect and make the word "Yahweh," as it might have been pronounced. No one was supposed to be pronouncing it anyway! Instead, they added the vowels from the substitute word, *Adonai*, Hebrew for "lord," to the consonants *YHWH*. The addition created, in print, a word that isn't an actual word but a hybrid of the two. Hebrew readers saw the hybrid word and knew to say *"Adonai."*

What To Do—Attempt Number 1: "Jehovah"

The way *YHWH* was written in the Hebrew text provided translators with an interesting problem, which they have handled in different ways over the years. To examine the question, let's first consider proper names in general.

Proper names get transliterated, not translated, and then modified. For example, this is what the name Moses looks like in the Hebrew characters with pointing (the dots above the rightmost letter and below the middle letter are the pointing).

מֹשֶׁה

When we transliterate, or write this name in the English alphabet, we get *Mosheh*. Then *Mosheh* is modified to give us the English version of the name, Moses. It's a two-step process—transliterate, then modify.

This is what the name *Yosheph* looks like.

יוֹסֵף

Hebrew reads from right to left, opposite of English, so when we see a word in the Hebrew characters, it's reversed in letter order. Notice this name begins with Y, which is the tiny letter on the right, י, that looks like an apostrophe. *Yosheph* is the English transliteration that is then modified to give us Joseph. This is a good example of how the Hebrew Y is usually rendered as a J in English. Likewise, W is often made into V.

In Hebrew characters (just the consonants), *YHWH* looks like this:

יהוה

Notice it begins (on the right) with the same small, apostrophe-looking Y letter as the name *Yosheph*. With the vowels for *Adonai*, it looks like this:

יְהוָֹה

For God's name, what should they do? They have the original letters *YHWH* and then the vowels from *Adonai*, so the translator sees something that looks like:

$Y^aH^oW^aH$

If you try to read that aloud as if it were a single word, and remember to make the Y into a J sound, and the W into a V sound, what do you get? Ja-ho-vah. This is the origin of the word "Jehovah." It isn't a real name—it was accidentally "created" by transliterating the divine name with the Hebrew consonants for *YHWH* plus the Hebrew vowels for *Adonai*. "Jehovah" was a very common interpretation of the name of God for a time, and it appeared in some translations. It's still quite familiar to us.

But now we understand $Y^aH^oW^aH$ does not say "Jehovah." $Y^aH^oW^aH$ is not even a real word—it is made of the consonants from one word and the vowels from another word. It's a hybrid. Since "Jehovah" is not an actual word in any manuscript, it is no longer used in most English translations.

What To Do—Attempt Number 2: "The LORD"

What should translators do instead? The most obvious thing would be to use an English version of a name made from the letters *YHWH*. Scholars have done a lot of work to decide that "Yahweh" would be the best English pronunciation of the name indicated by *YHWH*. So, translators could use "Yahweh," but they do not use Yahweh in most cases. Why not?

The answer comes from the Jewish practice of pronouncing *Adonai*, the Hebrew for "lord," when a reader came to the divine name in the Hebrew text. The Septuagint was the first to translate based on this tradition.

The Septuagint is the Greek translation of the
Hebrew Scriptures, produced by Jewish scholars
in Alexandria from the third to the second
century BC. It is an important translation that
was highly prevalent in the ancient world in the
time of Jesus and the apostles. In many cases we
can see in the New Testament scriptures that the
authors are quoting from the Septuagint rather
than from the original Hebrew. We can think
of the Septuagint as the Bible that Jesus and the
apostles used.

The translators who produced the Septuagint
took proper names in Hebrew and made them
into similar names in Greek. For example, the
Hebrew *Mosheh* looks like *Moseus* in Greek. A
transfer such as this one into the new language
is the normal thing to do with proper names.
The creators of the Septuagint could have made
a Greek name out of the letters for *YHWH*
by transliterating into Greek (and supplying
appropriate vowels). However, they did not
do that. Scripture readers never pronounced

YHWH aloud in Hebrew but said *Adonai*, the Hebrew for "lord." In Greek, the equivalent word for *Adonai*, or "lord," is *kurios*. The Septuagint translators just used the word *kurios* for every instance of *YHWH*.

The choice to replace *YHWH* with *kurios*, the Greek word for "lord," in the Septuagint produced a precedent that English translations have followed.

However, English translators didn't want to *just* use "lord" or "Lord" because that's already how the Hebrew word for lord, *Adonai*, is translated. They didn't want the personal name of God to disappear from the text. Translators wanted to distinguish *YHWH* from *Adonai* and indicate that the special, divine name is in the Hebrew text. For that, they needed some special formatting.

Translators decided on a special version of "LORD" with the distinctive small caps format. Thus, God's personal name is written as "the

LORD" every time the Hebrew text has *YHWH*. If a font does not have the small caps option, then the divine name is written in all caps, "the LORD"—it has the same meaning.

Do *all* English translations use this exact convention? Most do, but there is some variety—the American Standard Version and Young's Literal Translation still use Jehovah for a few instances of *YHWH*. The New Living Translation, World English, Names of God, and Lexham English Bibles use Yahweh occasionally and "the LORD" the rest of the time (for example the NLT uses "Yahweh" 11 times out of over 6,000 instances of *YHWH*). However, most English translations use "the LORD" consistently, including the most common translations—the New International Version, King James Version, English Standard Version, and New American Standard Bible.

Check out a few versions of the Bible. What do the passages above use for the name of

God in your translation(s)? What do you think about their choices? What is the most reverent choice? What is the clearest? It's hard to know what factors should be most important in our translations, whether reverence, clarity, closeness to original language, or tradition. We'd love to have all of the above! But translation is difficult and always involves some tradeoffs. Here we have a translation situation that took a whole chapter to explain! That makes it a good time to reflect on the way this particular word, the name of God, communicates to us about God. More about these ideas in our next chapter.

Key Scriptures for Chapter 2: "The Tetragrammaton and 'the LORD'"

Exodus 33:19
Exodus 34:6-7

Questions for Thought or Discussion:

> 1. Is it important to honor God's name as holy? Why or why not? What practices

around God's name communicate
reverence?

2. Do you or does your church tradition
use the name Jehovah? Why might
some people continue to use the name
Jehovah, even if it was not a real word?

3. How does your Bible translation
indicate the name of God? Is it with
capital letters? Small caps? Does your
Bible ever use "Yahweh?"

4. Look at your translation for Genesis
15:2. Below is how it reads in the
NASB.

2 Abram said, "O Lord GOD, what
will You give me, since I am
childless, and the heir of my house
is Eliezer of Damascus?" (Genesis
15:2, NASB)

Why do you think "GOD" is in small caps instead of Lord? What word must "Lord" be translating here? What word must "GOD" represent?

Chapter Three

Why Does it Matter?

5 Thus says God the LORD,
Who created the heavens and
stretched them out,
Who spread out the earth and its
offspring,
Who gives breath to the people on it
And spirit to those who walk in it,
6 "I am the LORD, I have called You
in righteousness,
I will also hold You by the hand and
watch over You,
And I will appoint You as a covenant
to the people,

As a light to the nations,
⁷ To open blind eyes,
To bring out prisoners from the
dungeon
And those who dwell in darkness
from the prison.

⁸ "I am the LORD, that is My
name…"

Isaiah 42:5-8a, NASB

We've spent a lot of time talking about one word in the Bible! Why does it matter? From the passage at the burning bush, I think we can see that the revelation of God's name mattered to God. If it mattered then, it still matters now, right?

The Meaning of the Name *YHWH*

The name of God communicates the nature of God. Knowing God's name helps us understand one aspect of who God is, that *YHWH* is not a contingent being. The great I AM is not dependent on anyone or anything to exist. When we begin to grasp this element of the nature of God, even if we can't grasp it fully, we are meeting a deep truth of reality. All of creation is God's… but God is not created. Everything we see is a layer of reality that is contingent on the ultimate reality, *YHWH*, the foundation and source of all being. God reveals this truth to us. When we search for ultimate reality, there is something to find: God and the truth of God's nature.

Did we get too philosophical? It's deep stuff! To know the name of the source of all existence is powerful. It isn't powerful in the way of "If I know your name I can compel you to grant my wishes." It's powerful in the sense of how we ground our understanding of what reality is: reality is *YHWH*. When we begin with God, we are connected to the source of all existence. And what we learn from God's revelation is that the source of reality is a person, not an impersonal force, and that person loves us deeply and unfailingly. Throughout Scripture, God announces God's name as a way of summing up God's character and the kind of actions God will take to love us and to rescue us, as in Isaiah 42 (above). It is so good!

The whole story of the Bible is God's revelation of God's self and God's purposes for creation. God reveals God's character and nature to us as humans—that's pretty amazing, isn't it? God even tells us God's personal name. We don't have to trick God into telling us so we can control God with an incantation. Instead, God reveals God's personal name to Moses, with instructions to share it. God places it throughout the Bible for every reader through the generations. God's sharing this name is a mark of relationship and connection. It is so good to know that a sovereign and powerful God wants to have a personal relationship with each human being personally and with humans as a community.

Many of us never knew that "the LORD" represented Yahweh or even that this word had a proper name behind it. We may have known that God is called "I AM" but not that "I AM" is the meaning of God's actual name. It's good to know that there is a name in the Scriptures. *YHWH,* or Yahweh, is the personal name of the one true God, the God of Abraham, Isaac, and Jacob.

Jesus and I AM

We've discussed how the name of God mattered to God in the Old Testament when God revealed the name Yahweh, or "I AM." The name of God also mattered to Jesus in his ministry on earth. Jesus drew on the name

"I AM" in his teaching about himself. In the gospel of John, Jesus makes seven "I am" statements about himself during his ministry:

I am the bread of life (John 6:35, 41, 48, and 51).
I am the light of the world (John 8:12).
I am the door of the sheep (John 10:7, 9).
I am the resurrection and the life (John 11:25).
I am the good shepherd (John 10:11, 14).
I am the way, the truth, and the life (John 14:6).
I am the true vine (John 15:1, 5).

These are some big claims! Jesus is telling us that he is the bread of our lives, the provision that sustains us. Jesus is the way, the truth, and the life: the one way to connect to the Father, the very reality in which we exist, and the essence of life itself. He is the good shepherd... because God promised in Ezekiel 34 that one day *God* would come and be the good shepherd. The content of these claims is huge—Jesus is our everything!

But look also at the wording of these claims: each one starts with the statement "I am." The repetition gives us a clue that this phrase of "I am" means something. Then, when we realize there are *seven* statements beginning with "I am," we start to understand that it is an intentional pattern. Jesus is using the "I am" part of these phrases to make another, special claim about his nature.

One additional "I am" statement helps us understand what that special claim is:

> [58] Jesus said to them, "Truly, truly, I say to you, before Abraham was born, **I am**." (John 8:58, NASB, emphasis added)

If we didn't know anything about the phrase "I am" in the history of Scripture, that would be a weird thing to say. What would it mean? First, we can reason that it means Jesus existed before

Abraham was born. And second, we can infer from Jesus' saying "I am" rather than "I was," that there is something timeless about Jesus' existence.

But we do know about the phrase "I am!" We know that it is the meaning of God's personal name! Jesus is claiming to exist, before Abraham, as the timeless, non-contingent God. Now Jesus' claim about himself is even BIGGER. Jesus is claiming to *be* God—to have the same identity, name, and eternal nature. Jesus is here to be the rescuing God, the God of love and promise-keeping, in person. He's here to rescue God's people again, as God did in the Exodus, this time rescuing each one of us from the power of evil and from slavery to sin.

Do you think Jesus meant to say all that? Are we reading more into the text than we should? Let's look at how Jesus' audience reacted:

> ^{59} Therefore they picked up stones to throw at Him, but Jesus hid Himself and went out of the temple. (John 8:59, NASB)

Wow, they were angry! But we have to know something about their culture to know how angry. Picking up stones to throw at him was not like throwing rotten tomatoes. It was the beginning of execution by stoning. Stoning, or throwing stones at the person until they died, was the form of capital punishment required for blasphemy, which was claiming equality with God. This claim of Jesus caused those listening to try to *kill* him. They were attempting to execute him for a religious crime, the crime of claiming the name of God for himself. Jesus' audience knew exactly the implication of Jesus' statement: that Jesus is the "I AM" of God.

All these "I am" statements in the gospel are written in ancient Greek, the language of the New Testament. Jesus probably spoke them in

Aramaic, the language of the common people, and then the authors of the gospels wrote them in Greek. So, none of these statements contained the Hebrew word "*YHWH*." But the meaning of *YHWH* carried through. It spoke to those who originally heard Jesus, to the first readers of the gospels, and it speaks to us today.

The name of God, "I AM WHAT I AM," or "I WILL BE WHAT I WILL BE" still speaks to us about God's nature, and the nature of Jesus the Son as God. It's very powerful!

Should we say Yahweh?

Now let's address a practical question. Even after we know all this compelling meaning of the name *YHWH*, we need to decide whether to say "Yahweh" or not.

Sometimes when I think of the goodness of God in revealing God's name to us, I feel a little sad that we don't always use the name Yahweh.

Should we? God gave it to us! He instructed Moses to use it, saying "tell them the LORD sent you," or "tell them *YHWH* sent you." And it's all over the Bible—over 6,000 uses!

The divine name is present even in the passages before the burning bush scene in Exodus 3 in which God reveals God's name as *YHWH*. This happens because the Hebrew Scriptures are a unified whole which was finalized *after* all the events they describe. Maybe that's an obvious statement—we know a story can't be finished until after the events it describes—but it has always been a helpful point for me. We know the Scriptures were put together in their final form with great intentionality and literary artistry. These final compilers of Hebrew Scriptures knew the name *YHWH* and used it throughout Scripture. "*YHWH*" is present as early as the creation stories (Gen. 2:4 is the first instance). The Scriptures use it, so it makes sense to ask, shouldn't we? Or, is it too holy to say aloud?

Some scholars and teachers do use the name
Yahweh. When the name was thought to
read "Jehovah" it was used regularly. If we say
Yahweh in reverence, there is nothing wrong
with using it. It isn't sacrilege, because God
made us to seek relationship with God. That
relationship includes learning to know God,
including God's name, in all God's holiness!
Using the name Yahweh is true to the intent
of Scripture, since the name *YHWH* is present
so many times. Scripture doesn't hesitate to use
YHWH or save it for special occasions. And
when we remember the meaning of the name
Yahweh and the story of God's revealing it,
it reminds us who God is. God is the great I
AM, an eternal being who is not contingent on
anyone or anything, who exists without being
created and without needing anything outside
of Yahweh to continue. Instead, Yahweh is the
source and foundation for our being!

On the other hand, there are reasons some
people choose not to use it. First, many people

are unfamiliar with the name Yahweh, so we could end up with a disconnect if people don't know who we are talking about.

Also, in the New Testament Jesus and the apostles did not use the Hebrew name "Yahweh," though Jesus did use "I am" statements to reveal his character and divinity. Jesus and the apostles used "Lord" like the Septuagint does. They also sometimes referred to God by titles (such as the "Blessed One" in Mark 14:61, NASB, or the "Power" in Mark 14:62, NASB), which was a common way Jews of that period spoke of God without saying God's name. Although Jesus did not say Yahweh, we know Jesus was teaching Jews at a time when none of them would say God's name aloud. It would have been horrifying to his audience for Jesus to speak the name "Yahweh."

However, we are not the same audience. We don't have the same culture as first century Jews. Just because Jesus didn't say Yahweh at that time doesn't mean he would not have done so in a different cultural atmosphere. Still, we may choose not to say Yahweh because Jesus didn't during his ministry.

In the present day, observant Jews do not say the name of God. They even write the word "God" as "G-d" as a mark of respect. We may choose not to say Yahweh out of respect for our Jewish friends.

In addition, when we say "Lord," as many generations of readers of the Hebrew text would have said, we're participating in a historically respectful tradition. But if we are reading "Lord" without knowing it has any additional meaning, that isn't respect or disrespect—it's just reading what's there. To participate consciously in that tradition, we need to know that "the Lord" stands for *YHWH*—then we can decide whether or not to say Yahweh aloud, and in what way we can show reverence.

The translators of our Scriptures mostly choose to use "the LORD," so when we read Scripture "the LORD" will already be in the text. But what should we say in our conversations about the Scripture and about God? Should we say "Yahweh" in those contexts?

There are good things about saying "LORD"—we'll be speaking of God as "LORD" as Jesus did in the gospels and the New Testament authors did in their writings. We'll be using the same tradition as the Septuagint, the translation that Jesus and the apostles used. And we'll be imitating a practice of reverential Judaism.

However, there are also good things about saying Yahweh, the name God intentionally revealed to us. To say "Yahweh" clarifies that God *has* a proper name. It honors God's revelation of the name of Yahweh in Scripture. It communicates that Yahweh is not interchangeable with other gods. And, it makes sense of passages in which God proclaims, "I am

Yahweh, that is my name" (Isaiah 42:8a, author's translation; compare to the NASB "I am the LORD, that is My name" in the NASB).

We can do either, or both (I do both), and keep growing closer to God. We want to reflect on God's greatness in being, and on God's goodness in love. One way to do that is to reflect on the divine name and God's revelation of it to us. Either way, knowing the name Yahweh is good!

Key Scriptures for Chapter 3: "Why Does it Matter?"

Isaiah 42:5-8a
Exodus 3:14-15
John 8:58-59

Questions for Thought or Discussion:

> 1. How would you explain the meaning of the name *YHWH*?

> 2. What does the non-contingency of

God mean to you? Is it highly meaningful? Too abstract? How does it relate to our nature as humans?

3. What does Jesus' use of "I am" mean for the nature of Jesus? Do you think Jesus meant to communicate everything we discussed about his being God by just the seven "I am" statements? What about the last statement, "before Abraham was born, I am" (John 8:58)?

4. Do you say the name Yahweh? Will you begin to say it?

5. How will you read Scripture differently now when you encounter verses that use "the LORD?"

Sources

This material comes from various instruction I've received and reading I've done over the years. I am now explaining from that knowledge base. But what instruction and what reading? The sources deserve to be credited, even if my memory of where the knowledge came from is imperfect. Thank you in particular to Dr. Mark Shipp for his Reading the Old Testament course and Hebrew courses. Thank you also to Dr. Daniel Napier for his insight into so many things, but here particularly the conceptual image of a bush that does not burn up, an "unfed fire." In addition, although I have not quoted from it, I regularly use a multi-author commentary set to develop understanding of passages. Thus, I am citing the Exodus volume of that commentary here.

Bruckner, James K. Exodus. Understanding the Bible Commentary Series. (eBook Edition, 2012 ed.). (R. L. W. Ward Gasque, Ed.) Grand Rapids, MI: Baker Books.

Napier, Daniel. "Soul Whisperer: Jesus' Way Among the Philosophers" (Manuscript in preparation for publication, received 10 March, 2023). p.62–64.

Shipp, R. Mark. "The United Kingdom." Reading the Old Testament, 5 October, 2016. Austin Graduate School of Theology, Austin, TX. Lecture.

Shipp, R. Mark. "Vowels." Introduction to Biblical Hebrew, 4 September, 2014. Austin Graduate School of Theology, Austin, TX. Lecture.

Acknowledgements

It takes a lot of steps to produce and publish even a very short book such as this one! My family has been asked to read, compare cover designs, and listen to my internal debates about how to do things, so thank you to my husband James and my sons Zack and Sam.

My first readers and editors are an amazing team of my sister, Julie Abels; my mother- and father-in-law, Linda and Daniel Munger; and my mom, Pam Emerson. I'm very blessed to have people of your editing skills in my family, but I'm even more thankful for you as sounding boards and constant sources of support. A special thank-you to Julie for constantly listening, for brainstorming with me, and for sharing your publishing experience and expertise.

Thank you to beta readers Amanda Pfeifer, Daren Allee, and Teri Wenck who made this book better with their ideas.

I deeply appreciate my theological education at Austin Graduate School of Theology and especially three professors who have continued to provide Biblical and theological discussion long afterwards, Todd Hall, Keith Stanglin, and Mark Shipp.

About the Author

Deanna Munger is a writer and teacher in Bible Study and theology. She is a Christian, wife, and mother of two teenage sons in Austin, Texas.

Deanna earned a BS in Chemical Engineering from the University of Arizona and worked in the Semiconductor industry for a number of years before having her two sons. After trying several jobs such as being an online math tutor, running a cake decorating business, and coordinating weddings for her church, she found herself taking classes at the Austin Graduate School of Theology (later Lipscomb University, Austin Center).

Deanna discovered that she loved the depth and transformative power of her seminary classes and went on to earn a Master of Arts degree in Theological Studies. Currently, Deanna teaches in-person classes at her local church and online classes for students from multiple Christian traditions and multiple time zones. Classes are open to new students and information can be found at DeannaMunger.com.

Deanna's other interests are in watercolor and alcohol ink art, reading science fiction and mystery novels, and trying to keep up with her outdoorsy husband and surprisingly athletic children. She is passionate about bringing the kind of substance and inspiration she found in her studies to YOU in the form of Bible studies, speaking events, and books.

Find more about Deanna and her work at DeannaMunger.com.

Connect with the Author

Thank you for taking the time to read this book.

For more books and for resources such as live and recorded Bible studies, please visit

DeannaMunger.com

and subscribe to my mailing list.

Do you have questions about the Bible, Bible study, or the Christian life? Do you want to discuss the material here or on my website?

This book was developed because of questions and comments I received from fellow students of the Word. I am always working on more books and studies like this one and the others on my website. If you have topics you would like to learn more about, please share them will me. You can message me using my website, DeannaMunger.com or by email at deanna.munger@gmail.com.

Get a Free E-book

If you would like to have an e-book copy of this study, subscribe to my website at

DeannaMunger.com

to get access to this title or another like it. E-books are available in multiple formats such as PDF, Kindle, Apple Books, and more.